Weekend Fun

Let's Go on a

Picnic

By Cate Foley

New Lenox
Public Library District
120 Veterans Parkway
New Lenox, Illinois 60451

Children's Press
A Division of Scholastic Inc.
New York / Toronto / London / Auckland / Sydney
Mexico City / New Delhi / Hong Kong
Danbury, Connecticut

Photo Credits: Cover and all photos by Maura Boruchow
Contributing Editors: Jeri Cipriano, Jennifer Silate
Book Design: Victoria Johnson

Visit Children's Press on the Internet at:
http://publishing.grolier.com

Library of Congress Cataloging-in-Publication Data

Foley, Cate.
  Let's go on a picnic / by Cate Foley.
    p. cm. — (Weekend fun)
  Includes bibliographical references and index.
  ISBN 0-516-23189-8 (lib. bdg.) -- ISBN 0-516-29579-9 (pbk.)
    1. Picnicking--Juvenile literature. [1. Picnicking.] I. Title. II. Series.

GT2955 .F6 2001
642'.3--dc21

00-050869

3 1984 00218 0477

Contents

We are going on a **picnic** at lunchtime today.

I help make the food.

4

We go to the park.

6

We spread our blanket on the grass.

9

We are ready to eat.

The food looks **delicious**.

I eat a **sandwich**.

Belle has a dog biscuit.

14

15

After lunch, we play ball.

16

We clean up before we leave.

We throw away the **garbage**.

18

19

We had a good day.

Our picnic was fun.

21

New Words

delicious (dih-**lihsh**-uhs) something
that tastes good

garbage (**gar**-bihj) things that you
throw away

picnic (**pihk**-nihk) a meal eaten outdoors

sandwich (**sand**-wihch) food between
two pieces of bread

To Find Out More

Books

Packing for a Picnic
by Lorraine Long
Periwinkle Park Educational Productions

We Had a Picnic This Sunday Past
by Jacqueline Woodson
Disney Press

Web Site

Sesame Street Parents Magazine: Sesame Workshop
http://www.ctw.org/parents/familypicnic
This Web site has seasonal recipes and
picnic ideas for the whole family.

Index

About the Author

Cate Foley writes and edits books for children. She lives in New Jersey with her husband and son.

Reading Consultants

Kris Flynn, Coordinator, Small School District Literacy, The San Diego County Office of Education

Shelly Forys, Certified Reading Recovery Specialist, W.J. Zahnow Elementary School, Waterloo, IL

Sue McAdams, Certified Reading Recovery Specialist and Literary Consultant, Dallas, TX